If you knew, without a doubt, that you could get anything you want in life, if you just gave enough to others, you would probably ponder, **"How can I give more?"**

The Giving Journal addresses this one question ... **"How can you give more to others?"**

Read on ... Giving more (and then ultimately getting more) has never been simpler.

THE GIVING JOURNAL

Achieving Success Through Focused Generosity

FRANK AGIN
Author of *Foundational Networking*

418 PRESS

THE GIVING JOURNAL

Achieving Success Through Focused Generosity

FRANK AGIN

Author of *Foundational Networking*

If you knew, without a doubt, that you could get anything you want in life, if you just gave enough to others, you would probably ponder, "How can I give more to other people?"

The Giving Journal addresses this one question ... How can you give more to others?

Read on ... giving more (and then ultimately getting more) has never been more simple.

Frank Agin is the author of *Foundational Networking: Building Know, Like and Trust To Create A Lifetime of Extraordinary Success*, and co-author of *LinkedWorking: Generating Success on the World's Largest Professional Networking Website* and *The Champion: Finding the Most Valuable Person in Your Network*.

THE GIVING JOURNAL ™

FRANK AGIN
Author of *Foundational Networking*

Copyright © 2012 by Frank Agin. All rights reserved.

Printed in the United States of America

Permission to reproduce or transmit in any form or by any means, electronic or mechanical, including photocopying and recording, or by an information storage and retrieval system, must be obtained by writing to the author, Frank Agin. He may be contacted at the following address:

AmSpirit
BUSINESS CONNECTIONS
Post Office Box 30724
Columbus, Ohio 43230
Toll free: (888) 267-7474
Email: frankagin@amspirit.com

Proofreading: Linda Agin
Editing & Interior Design:
Stephanie Donavan & Kim Mettille
Book Cover and Graphic Design:
Kim Mettille

Ordering Information:
To order additional copies, contact 418 PRESS.

ISBN: 978-0-9823332-3-5

Published by: 418 PRESS
A Division of Four Eighteen Enterprises LLC

Dedication

Dedicated to all those ambitious, courageous and hardworking men and women of AmSpirit Business Connections who believe what I believe ... that what you get out of life grows immensely when you focus on giving to others.

THE GIVING JOURNAL

Table of Contents

Foreword	1
A Case For Giving	7
The Focus On Giving More	19
From Weight Loss To Networking	31
The Science Behind *The Giving Journal*	39
Making A Tally; Not Keeping Score	43
Not All Giving Is Equal	51
Working The Giving Journal	59
What Is Not Giving	63
What To Give? What To Give?	67
Tracking (or Not) Insignificant Giving	77
Thoughts From Social Media	81

THE GIVING JOURNAL

Foreword

People can be classified in lots of different ways ... short or tall ... ambitious or unmotivated ... leader or follower. One seldom used classification, however, is "net giver" or "net taker."

Net takers are those who seem to get more from the world than they put into it. They get referrals, but never seem to give them. People connect "net takers" to others, but they seem to be oblivious to the fact that they could benefit others in the same way. They gather information from those around them, but are tight lipped about things they may know.

Worst of all, "net takers" do not seem to care about this imbalance (and in some instances they pride themselves on it).

Net givers on the other hand, seem to not only give more to the world than they take from it, they focus on giving referrals whenever they can. In addition, they go out of their way to connect people in their network. They readily share information to whomever they believe could benefit from it. Best of all, "net givers" seem to truly delight in finding ways to serve others and seldom (if ever) wonder what might be coming back to them.

The contrast between "net takers" and "net givers" is interesting. More than being interesting, however, it comes with a wonderful irony, that over time those who focus on giving end up getting immensely more from those around them, than those who focus on getting.

The "net takers" develop a reputation that is far from desirable and repulsive in nature. As such, they are on an endless search to find new situations where they can take, but not give (or at least not as much) in return. These circumstances, however, are few and far between. And even when the "net taker" finds one it never lasts long, as people move on generally feeling cheated or fleeced.

In contrast, "net givers" develop an aura of altruism that is seemingly magnetic. As a result, quality others search them out in droves. More often than not, the people they attract come intending to develop lasting relationships. These ongoing associations are forged together with a continual flow of referrals, contacts and information. From here, although the "net giver" shares plenty, they get much in return.

Being a "net giver" is immensely more profitable, productive and rewarding than a "net taker" could ever imagine. Those that pride themselves on giving know this. As such, they search tirelessly for ways to give more. For the true "net giver," *The Giving Journal* is one more arrow in the quiver to embracing a life-long giving mentality.

JOURNAL

Date   Act of Giving

THE GIVING JOURNAL

A Case For Giving

> "If America is the pursuit of happiness, the best way to pursue happiness is to help other people."
>
> **George Lucas**
> Screenwriter & Producer

Why do you network? Why do you interact with those around (or those literally around the world via social media)?

While you might have a more specific answer, generally you network because those around you (or contacts on the far reaches of planet Earth) provide you with benefits – opportunities, information, support, and energy as well as additional contacts. Think about it. Everything you have, anywhere you have been, and all you are is a function of these benefits. The benefits of networking have literally built your life.

You no doubt wonder "how can I parlay my networking into getting myself more of the good things I want and need?" This is the ultimate question in networking. While meeting and interacting with all sorts of interesting and wonderful people is great in and of itself, at some point you look for a return on your investment of time and energy. Certainly, your interest in answering this question motivates you to read volumes of books and articles on networking and drives you to attend seminars (whether in person or online) on the subject.

The answer to the question of how do you improve the flow of benefits to you from networking is really very simple. To get benefits from your networking efforts, you first need to provide these benefits to others in your network. Yes, although counterintuitive, the mantra of successful networking can be summed up in three words: *Give, Give, Give.*

Ask anyone who knows anything about networking and they will tell you that the fastest, easiest, and simplest way to get from your network is to give to it first – and give to it often. This is true whether you are networking for personal or professional reasons.

While you are certainly ever hopeful of getting from your network, the only thing you truly have control over is what you give. Therefore, you are best to focus your energies on what you contribute and simply trust that the "Get" portion of life will take care of itself.

In networking, giving will jump start an ailing network. If the productivity of your network leaves something to be desired, focus some attention on contributing to those around you and you will detect a noticeable up-tick in what comes back to you.

In networking, giving is the great equalizer. If you focus hard enough on contributing to those around you, you can overcome most any deficiency (such as talent, intelligence and charisma). Once you overcome the deficiency, you will benefit just as much as anyone else.

In networking, giving is the trump card. Everything else being equal, if you are better focused on contributing to those around you, you will simply get more from your networking efforts than others.

In each situation, giving to your network is not only the right thing to do from a moral perspective, but it also sets in motion psychological forces that almost compel others people to give, which ultimately will benefit you.

The benefits to you have many facets. In experimentation, social scientists have proved three wonderful benefits of giving. First, when you give to someone, they feel an underlying compulsion to give back.

Known as reciprocity, this phenomenon has occurred time after time in human existence. You can probably recollect examples from your own experiences. In fact, the notion of reciprocity has been demonstrated in various social science experiments.

For example, in 2002 in the *Journal of Applied Social Psychology* (32: 300-309), behavioral scientist David Strohmetz and colleagues reported that in their study restaurant servers could increase the amount of tips they received by giving each patron an "after dinner" mint or two when they brought the bill.

It is important to note that the effects of reciprocity do not necessarily manifest themselves immediately. Consider the case of Mexico as documented by Robert Cialdini, Ph.D. in his book *Instant Influence* (1995

Dartnell). In 1990, after Mexico City suffered a disastrous earthquake, the government of Mexico received a $5,000 contribution from Ethiopia, despite the fact that this small African nation was in the midst of a terrible famine where on a daily basis its people were literally dying by the hundreds. Why would Ethiopia not keep the $5,000 for use with its own people? When asked this same question, the Ethiopian Relief Agency simply responded, "In 1935, when Italy invaded, Mexico *helped* us."

Donna Fisher, in her book *People Power* (1995 Bard & Stephen), refers to reciprocity as the "Boomerang Effect." According to Fisher, taking the initiative to give, participate and offer support to your network is similar to throwing a boomerang.

Eventually what you inject into your network – opportunities, information, support, energy and additional contacts – comes back to you.

So, not only is giving the right thing to do for others, but it is also a great thing to do for you and those around you. Researchers have demonstrated that when you give, your actions become somewhat contagious. When individuals in a study were treated to generosity, they seemed to become inspired to give to others.

This inspiration, however, was not limited to the direct recipients of generosity. Even those who witnessed the generosity from one person to another became more likely to be generous. *Connected: The Surprising Power Of Our Social Networks*

(James H. Fowler & Nicholas A. Christakis; Little, Brown & Company (2009)).

While this might not seem to have a benefit on you, think about it. When you give to someone, you inspire that person to give (as well as those who witness the act of generosity). This inspired person (or even persons) then gives to Person A. These same psychological forces then take hold within Person A.

This person is then inspired and gives to Person B. Then Person B, now generously inspired, gives to Person C. Take important note, however, you might be Person C (or even B or D, E, etc.). The point is that your generosity will ultimately make it back to you in some form or fashion.

It may not come directly from the person you originally gave to (which is why we should never expect something), but in a sense your giving sets in motion your own good fortune. This is certainly not perfect and hardly predicable, but certainly giving (as opposed to doing nothing) improves the odds that good things come to you.

Researchers have also demonstrated that when you are generous you release into your system a healthy dose of *oxytocin*, a powerful "feel-good" chemical that the body naturally produces.

This chemical is often referred to in science as the "human bonding" drug. When someone experiences love, their body releases *oxytocin* into their system pulling them towards their prospective mate. This same chemical floods a woman's system after child birth, motivating her to feel an incredibly strong attraction towards her child.

The benefits of *oxytocin* go beyond attracting you to another, however. It seems that this chemical serves to lower your levels of stress and improve your immunity. This is likely why science has proven that generous people are likely to enjoy a longer, healthier life (as opposed to those who are less generous). *Being Generous* (Theodore Malloch; Templeton Press (2009)).

In summary, while others certainly benefit from your generosity, so do you. Giving is simply a powerful business builder, a network enhancer, and a good health elixir.

THE GIVING JOURNAL

The Focus On Giving More

> "The miracle is this - the more we share, the more we have."
>
> **Leonard Nimoy**
> Actor

In plain English, when you give to others you reap loads of wonderful benefits. The world offers example after example of this – the most compelling of which is that it is the only certain way to have a productive network.

If you are like most people, however, once you surrender to the notion that giving is the fastest, easiest and simplest way to create a productive network, you begin to wonder, "How can I give more?" After all, you are smart. Once you discover how to make something work, you are going to undertake those success-driving activities.

When it comes to giving more to those around you, there are no secrets, tricks or magic. The key is to simply focus attention on the activity, as your energy will follow your attention. That is, as you focus on opportunities to give, you will literally find more opportunities to give.

Just telling yourself that you will focus more attention on it, however, falls under the category of "easier said than done." Stop for a moment and focus all of your attention on the many ways you can give to others. Think about that and nothing else.

Now hold that thought. It is hard. Other thoughts intervene – that proposal where you are trying to get the wording just right ... your evening or weekend plans ... even thinking about what you are going to do for lunch. And this is over just a few seconds.

Maintaining focus just gets more difficult when seconds become minutes and then hours or days. Making this more difficult is that not only do other thoughts intervene, so do other activities – telephone calls, meetings and other needs of a busy life.

Before long, other thoughts and activities consume your limited attention. These obligations of mind and action soon take priority. Before you know it, you are no longer focused at all on giving to those around you (even though you might tell yourself, "I will get back to that, right after I am done with this.").

This is not to say that you never give to others. You are just not focused on it in an intentional manner. When an opportunity presents itself (e.g., someone asks for a contribution) you give. Beyond that, however, giving to others likely just slips your mind. You are no longer focused on finding occasions to be generous with your time, talent, or resources.

The point is that focusing one's attention on giving to others on an ongoing basis is a tremendous challenge. This is, however, nothing unusual. You have lots going on in your life (career, family and other obligations plus personal pursuits) and as a result lots going on in your mind.

This is really no different than the dilemma many face relative to personal fitness. In the simplest terms, your weight is not what it was in high school or college. Life has been busy and working out has not been a priority. You find that you are carrying (to be kind) a few extra pounds. Now if you are not a fan of (or have failed at) fad diets, weight loss gimmicks or medical procedures, you are left with the most basic approach to getting your weight down: Focus on eating sensibly – reasonable portions of healthy food.

Now many people try this (one of whom might be you) and many of those people find that this so-called "focus" leaves their situation largely unchanged. While they may feel good about the effort, they are frustrated that their weight is largely unchanged.

It was not that logic behind the approach. The approach is sound. The problem is a matter of focus. Just telling yourself that you are going to focus attention on eating sensibly is not enough.

Sure, you can tell yourself that you are going to eat sensibly. On day one, you have a handle on things. You make all the right choices for breakfast, lunch and dinner plus limit your snacking. Day Two and Three might be the same – rock solid focus. This may even last for a week or two.

Eventually, you stray from your focus. You might innocently lose track – in a weak moment you eat the wrong thing or perhaps too much of the right thing. Or you might compromise your resolve – you justify to yourself, "I have been good and even gotten lots of exercise ... I am entitled to this burger, shake, and fries."

This loss of focus may not happen all at once. It might come in stages. For example, you might maintain focus all week long, but get seriously off track on the weekend. Or perhaps, you do great focusing on healthy eating for breakfast and lunch, but it is dinner and late night snacking that does you in.

Eating more sensibly is the most effective means of controlling your weight. Simple. Focusing on doing it, however, is another story.

And giving to others is the best way to develop your personal and professional network. Focusing on doing it, however, makes the execution of something simple much more challenging.

The point is, however, that just telling yourself that you are going to focus on eating sensibly or (for the purposes of this book) giving to others will not work long term. As a human you have too many competing interests. After all, it is counterintuitive to think that by giving more, you will get more. Plus, living in a civilized society, you have too many distractions.

So what is the answer? If giving to others is a great means of advancing your personal and professional networking, but simply telling yourself "I am really going to focus on giving more" is not effective long term, how can you become more consistent and proficient with your generosity?

The simple answer is "journal" it. That is, if you want to give more, by keeping an ongoing log of what you have given, your tendency will be to give more.

This is a natural tendency and does not only apply to your generosity. If you journalize what you eat you would be far more successful at managing your weight than if you merely tried to focus on eating the right type and amount of food. This is because like most people you tend to underestimate the amount of calories you ate. You rationalize your eating much like, "it's only a bagel." You then, of course, do not realize that just a bagel adds 290 calories. And even if you knew that a bagel is 290 calories, you likely could not keep track of all the calories you consumed before or after it over the course of a day.

With a journal, you would need to know that a bagel is 290 calories. Likewise, you would know what else you ate and the amount of calories it all had. The journal serves as a constant reminder as to what your focus is – eating the right type and amounts of food.

JOURNAL

Date   Act of Giving

THE GIVING JOURNAL

From Weight Loss To Networking

> "The trick in life is not figuring out what you can get, but what you can give."
>
> **Susan Jeffers**
> Author & Speaker

Journaling is effective in helping people eat the right type and amounts of food. Does that mean a similar approach might help you keep a focus on giving to others? Why not?

Even the most knowledgeable exercise and dietary professionals likely would be challenged by trying to maintain a focus on eating the right type of and amounts of food over time. If you are a mere novice, you do not stand a chance.

The same goes for networking. This is not about expertise, knowledge, or understanding. It is about focus. Even if you profess to live by "The Golden Rule of Networking" – to get from your network, you have to give to it first – you are only human. There are limits to your ability to focus and maintain attention on giving to others. That is, even if you want to be more attentive to contributing to the lives of others, you have distractions like anyone else.

Therefore, you might be missing lots of opportunities to be altruistic. If you want to challenge that, answer this: What did you do today to help another? How about yesterday? What are the ten things you did this week (or even five)? Last week? Month?

It is probably difficult to remember, isn't it? You might remember the big things, but the little things tend to fade from memory. And much of your contribution to the world around you is likely comprised on little things (after all, you cannot make the big gifts everyday).

Now I consider myself as having a firm grasp of networking and understand that the quintessential element for creating a successful network is giving to others. After all, my career and business is centered on writing and talking about and coaching others on generating more success from professional networking.

Despite this, I found it a challenge to maintain a focus on generosity. With that realization, I began keeping a journal or log of all the things I did for others – A Giving Journal. I would simply make a note each time I did anything of reasonable significance for another.

When I took someone to lunch, I would make a note of it. When I gave someone a copy of my book, I would do the same. I did likewise when I took time to meet with someone to discuss their resume' or business plan.

Through journaling, did I give more than before I started the process? There is no question that I do (and you would too). While I do admit that I have nothing concrete to compare my current level of giving to, there are three reasons why the process of journaling my giving helped me give more (and more importantly why it would help you too).

First, having the journal serves as a constant reminder that you should be giving to others. Whether it sits on your desk or you carry it with you daily, the journal is a tool to help keep your attention on finding opportunities to give to others. With greater attention to the activity of giving, you will have greater production on that activity.

Second, with a journal you will have a tally of generous acts. This will spur you to give more in two ways. One, the journal will alert you to giving slumps and encourage you out of them. By having the journal you will know that "I have not done anything for anybody today (or this week) I need to really search for ways to help others.". Two, the journal will help you take your giving to new heights. By journaling, you will know that "Today, I have had seven giving acts. If I can complete three more, I will have a new personal record."

Third, when you do something for another (no matter what it is), you feel great – the release of *oxytocin* in your system. This feeling spurs you on to perform other acts of generosity. With the journal, you can actually look back at all the giving you have done and spur yourself on to more and more.

JOURNAL

Date	Act of Giving

THE GIVING JOURNAL

The Science Behind *The Giving Journal*

"I think I began learning long ago that those who are happiest are those who do the most for others."

Booker T. Washington,
Educator & Author

Again there are no secrets, tricks or magic to keeping a Giving Journal. There are scientific reasons, however, as to why this sort of journaling works. The science behind *The Giving Journal* involves simple human behavior, which is part of human DNA as social science has demonstrated.

Since the dawn of the Industrial Revolution, the corporate world has sought to improve itself. To achieve this improvement, businesses would commission studies to find ways of enhancing the bottom line.

One such study was the Hawthorne Experiments. From 1927 to 1932, Professor Elton Mayo examined the relationship between productivity and working conditions at the Western Electric Hawthorne Works in Cicero, Illinois, near Chicago. Mayo started these experiments by examining how lighting affected productivity.

When Mayo increased the brightness of the lights, productivity increased. When he increased it again, productivity further increased. This pattern continued for several more trials. Mayo and the executives of Western Electric were excited as they felt they were on to something.

Then Mayo broke from the trend he was following and he dimmed the lights on the Western Electric employees. To his astonishment, productivity increased again. He immediately revised his hypothesis. The brightness of the lights did not affect productivity of workers. What affected the productivity of the workers was the mere fact that someone was monitoring and measuring their productivity. This became known as "The Hawthorne Effect."

When you journalize what and how much you eat The Hawthorne Effect is at work. While it may only be you, nevertheless someone is monitoring and measuring the activity. That action, in and of itself, is enough to keep you focused on the desired action – eating sensibly.

The same is true with *The Giving Journal*. While it may only be you doing the monitoring, if you effectively journal what you give, someone is in fact monitoring and measuring your altruism. That someone is you. By the very nature of the Hawthorne Effect, you will be focused on giving and as a result give more.

In addition, *The Giving Journal* helps you keep in perspective the extent to which you are giving to others. According to behavioral scientist Francis Flynn, over time, people tend to overestimate the value and extent of what they give to others (*Organizational Behavior and Human Decision Processes* 2003 91:38-50). With *The Giving Journal*, what you have given to others is logged and ready for you to reflect upon.

THE GIVING JOURNAL

Making A Tally Not Keeping Score

"Don't judge each day by the harvest you reap, but by the seeds you plant."

Robert Louis Stevenson,
Novelist

Granted, as a society, we are obsessed with keeping score. Keeping score is a natural part of most any athletic competition. In fact, we would be hard pressed to find a sporting event anywhere in the world that does not have some sort of tally system to keep track of who is ahead and ... well, who is not.

The fact of the matter is that keeping score is not just part of sports, it is vital to them. Without the score, we might as well just be fooling around with a ball in the backyard. It is the score itself that tells us whether we should adhere to the planned strategy, stall for victory, or press for a comeback.

The whole notion of keeping score has made its way into our daily lives as well. In the business world there is the Dow Jones Industrial Average, housing starts and Consumer Price Index. Each of these is akin to keeping score.

Closer to home than these measures of macroeconomics, there is still the notion of keeping score. Some of us contend with sales records, others focus on production quotas, or even the number of days without injury.

Keeping score is a natural part of our personal and professional lives. Despite this, we should never allow any notion of keeping score to become part of our daily networking activities. That is, we should not tally, track, or score how much we have done for anyone in comparison to anyone else with whom we interact.

First of all, it is important to stress that in networking when you give, you need to do so without expectation. That is, you should not do something for another and then wait for them to reciprocate (or worse yet, imply to them that they have an obligation to do so).

The "give without expectation" mantra, simply cannot happen when you try to keep score. Attempting to tally and track *who* has done what for us relative to what *we* have done for them, simply flies in the face of the notion of "giving and expecting nothing in return."

Even beyond this basic concept of recommended networking practices, keeping score of who does what as we interact with those around us is simply impractical. We each have hundreds of contacts and no two of those acquaintances are the same. The human brain is simply not equipped to compartmentalize and compute all the data.

Even if we could, how do we go about keeping score? How do we even begin to quantify the value of one referral, introduction, or kernel of information to another? The value of some things has an immediate apparent benefit. On the other hand, for some things the value may not manifest itself for years to come.

Furthermore, what we give in the realm of networking does not deplete us. After all, referrals, introductions and information do not take money from our pocket. For the most part, these things have no value to us. So what does it matter what we might get in return? Even if we could quantify the tally of "who has done what," why would we? As the exchange in any good networking relationship ebbs and flows, the score could never possibly be "all tied up."

As a result, part of the time, we would be ahead in the count – getting more than we have given. This would likely leave us feeling a sense of guilt. The other part of the time, you would be behind – not getting as much as we have given. Then we would likely waste energy with feelings of animosity.

With all of that, does *The Giving Journal* fly in the face of the notion that in networking you should not keep score? The simple answer is, "absolutely not."

The intent of *The Giving Journal* is to serve as a personal log of what you have done for others. By keeping this log, you focus more on giving to others. It is not intended (and you should never use it) as a means of tallying what you have done for others in comparison to what they have done for you.

Again, the notion behind *The Giving Journal* is to keep you focused on contributing to the lives of others. At the same time, in the true spirit of networking, as you fill your journal with all sorts of wonderful acts and activities, you just need to trust that those generous deeds will find their way back to you somehow, someway.

Certainly there are some who will contend that "you are only giving because you want to make an entry in your journal." So what? SO WHAT!? As long as you are not expecting something from someone else, what does it matter what prompts or motivates you to give.

THE GIVING JOURNAL

Not All Giving Is Equal

> "No act of kindness, no matter how small, is ever wasted."
>
> **Aesop**
> Greek Fabulist

This book is about "giving." It is about helping you create a heightened sense of generosity. This begs the question: Are you generous?

No doubt, you answer a confident "yes" to that question. Hopefully, you wouldn't seriously declare yourself anything less. Certainly, you can point to something you did to support your assertion that you are a benevolent individual.

Putting your own situation aside, however, is someone truly generous just because he or she did something generous at some point in his or her life? The answer is no, not necessarily.

If the answer is no, then, where is the line drawn? That is, at what point does someone become generous? If one act of giving does not make them generous, would two do it? How about three? Four?

Maybe it is not the quantity, but the quality. Is it the magnitude of the gift? Does a $1,000,000 gift make a person generous? Is someone giving $1,000,000 ten times more generous than someone giving $100,000? Again, the answer is no, not necessarily.

However, if the answer is no, then how much more or is it more?

Maybe it is a quality test, but the test is relative. Do we determine whether someone is generous by the magnitude of giving relative to what he or she has to offer? Could someone making a $10,000 gift be just as generous as someone giving a $1,000,000 gift? We would probably all agree that the answer is, maybe.

The fact of the matter is that the determination as to whether someone is generous is not absolute. That is, there is not a clear line separating those who are generous and those who are not. One act of giving over a lifetime does not necessarily make someone generous, but the act still represents generosity.

And even among people who are truly generous, there is a degree of disparity.

There are of people who are generous out of a sense of obligation. And there are people who are generous simply because it is the right thing to do. It is probably no revelation that there are varying degrees or types of generosity.

Author Julie Salamon addresses this notion in her book *Rambam's Ladder*. Salamon details the works of Rabbi Moses ben Maimon, known as Rambam, who, as part of his teachings, detailed different levels of charity. This 12th century physician, philosopher and scholar identified eight distinct levels of giving.

According to Rambam's Ladder, sometimes we begrudgingly give ("Okay ... alright ... here you go.") and other times we happily give, but do not give in an amount that we probably could. There are times when someone needs to be asked to give and sometimes we give of our own volition. There are times where we give, but want credit for it and sometimes our gifts are completely anonymous.

No, not all giving is equal. Giving comes in various amounts and with a variety of motivations and attitudes. Nevertheless, all giving represents generosity. In fact, everyone has some modicum of generosity, even the legendary Ebenezer Scrooge.

So to answer the questions in the opening paragraph of this section: Are you generous? The answer should be a resounding, YES. The purpose of this book, however, is really about answering another question: Are you committed to becoming more generous? With respect to that question, only time will tell.

JOURNAL

Date   Act of Giving

THE GIVING JOURNAL

Working *The Giving Journal*

"Life isn't just about what you can have; it's about what you have to give."

Oprah Winfrey
Television Host & Producer

Based on the successes that people find with respect to eating sensibly (as well as exercise, investing, and even marketing), journaling is just common sense. It is common sense, but it is not common practice.

Think about it. How much journaling do you do? Do you journal your caloric consumption? Maybe. Do you keep a record of your workouts? Again, maybe.

If you do, then you understand the power to it. Extend that practice to your giving. If you do not, then consider taking a leap of faith and trying it.

This journaling can be something that you commit to on an ongoing basis – amassing pages and pages or volumes and volumes of generous entries. This journaling can be something you commit to here or there. For example, you could designate a particular month (or week) as your "giving" month – a period of time where you use journaling as a method of really focusing on ramping up your generosity.

Whatever the case, there is no magic to the notion of a Giving Journal. You can journal in the pages of the printed version of this book. You can simply use a small lined record book (or even just note cards). You can keep your journal in an electronic format. Whatever you use, whenever you do something reasonably significant for someone else, briefly log it with the date.

THE GIVING JOURNAL

What Is Not Giving

> "Let no one ever come to you without leaving better and happier."
>
> **Mother Teresa**
> Missionary

It is also important to discuss what altruism is not. From time to time, you may hear someone make (or you might have made) a statement similar to, "I love what I do because I get to help people."

A great enthusiasm towards what one does is a powerful thing. It ensures that the business or profession serves its customers or clients at an exceptionally high level. However, when people look to serve those around them through the goods and services they sell – no matter how passionate they might be about it – it is not altruistic. This is business passion.

In reality, this passionate servicing of clients is nothing more than sales or client service. Nevertheless, no matter how much passion someone injects into the process of servicing customers and clients, sales or client service is simply providing someone pleasure or alleviating pain *through the goods or services they have to offer*.

True giving, however, is not what you have to sell, no matter how much benefit someone derives. Unless it is done at an extreme discount (or even a loss), a commercial transaction for goods or services is not giving.

Giving is doing something beneficial where you have absolutely no expectation of getting something in return, except for perhaps that warm and fuzzy feeling inside or the underlying belief that in the long term good will come to you.

THE GIVING JOURNAL

What To Give? What To Give?

> "You have it easily in your power to increase the sum total of this world's happiness now. How? By giving a few words of sincere appreciation to someone who is lonely or discouraged."
>
> **Dale Carnegie**
> Writer & Lecturer

When someone mentions the notion of "giving" does your mind begin to conjure up images of reaching for your wallet?

If you are like most anyone, you are envisioning yourself doling out money, whether cash, check or via plastic. You contribute to your favorite charity. You contribute to church. You contribute whenever someone passes the hat for a worthy cause.

This is great. These offerings constitute giving and you ought to appropriately note it in your version of *The Giving Journal*.

Giving, however, is not limited to the dollars and cents you bestow upon others. Rather for purposes of *The Giving Journal*, giving involves the entire universe of generosity. This can be divided into three main sub-headings or areas of capital: Physical Capital, Human Capital and Social Capital.

Physical Capital: This includes financial assets like money, real estate, or stocks, but it also encompass all of the other things you own (cars, clothing, collections, etc).

- **Have you contributed to that cause that is close to your heart?** No matter how little you feel you have, there is someone with less. Anything you can contribute would be appreciated.
- **Have you donated vehicles and other items to charity organizations?** While your cash situation may be tight, no doubt you have many useful things that other organizations can use or convert to cash.
- **Have you given items to others that are no longer a use to you,**

but that have great use for someone else? Perhaps you no longer golf or your kids have outgrown those football cleats. If there is still life in the items, you can find someone to put them to use.

Human Capital: This is your ability to accomplish things with the 24 hours you have each day and is not just your time, but also your underlying talents and abilities.

- **Have you spent time on the telephone, via e-mail or in person providing guidance or sincerely listening?** While it would be difficult to identify its impact on the bottom line, there is a tremendous benefit in spurring someone on when things just have not gone their way.

- **Have you shared information you have or insight in an area where you are a subject-matter expert?** A link to an insightful website, a tip on a special government training program, or advice on accounts receivable collection are just a few ideas that could certainly serve to benefit others.
- **Have you served on a volunteer board or contributed time to a worthwhile charitable or**

civic cause? In addition to financial contribution, not-for-profit and community organizations need your time and talent.

- **Have you taken time to help someone with their resumé or business plan?** Information that can give someone an inside track or competitive advantage is often as valuable as "cold, hard cash."

Social Capital: These are all the people in your life that you know and are connected to and represent your ability to motivate, influence and draw upon these people in your life.

- **Have you introduced someone in your network to another?** While introductions to new customers and clients are wonderful, introductions to potential business or strategic partners, quality employees, and even reliable vendors also have tremendous value.

- **Have you shared someone's business plan (or resumé) with people who might find it of interest?** Having a sound business plan or stellar personal credentials is of little value unless they find their way into the hands of someone in which they matter. If you make that connection, you potentially give a fortune.

- **Have you referred someone in your network to another?** The next best thing to giving someone money is referring them to someone who will (for goods or services that is).

JOURNAL

Date   Act of Giving

————   ——————————————————————
————   ——————————————————————
————   ——————————————————————
————   ——————————————————————
————   ——————————————————————
————   ——————————————————————
————   ——————————————————————
————   ——————————————————————
————   ——————————————————————
————   ——————————————————————
————   ——————————————————————
————   ——————————————————————
————   ——————————————————————
————   ——————————————————————
————   ——————————————————————
————   ——————————————————————
————   ——————————————————————
————   ——————————————————————
————   ——————————————————————
————   ——————————————————————

THE GIVING JOURNAL

Tracking (Or Not) Insignificant Giving

> "Think of giving not as a duty but as a privilege."
>
> **John D. Rockefeller Jr.**
> Industrialist & Philanthropist

The Giving Journal is a powerful means of keeping you focused on giving to others. The journaling aspect (the actual writing down of giving activity) should almost be a celebration of your generosity. That is, you should look forward to the action of putting in writing the treasure, time or talent that you have given to another.

The journaling, however, should not be a chore. If it becomes that, you will find yourself not keeping tabs on what you have given. When that happens, the power of *The Giving Journal* is impaired.

This is not to say that you should only focus on giving in matters that allow you to make an entry in your journal. You should take every opportunity to give to the world around you, but use your best judgment as to whether it warrants you time to enter your act of generosity or thoughtfulness.

So perhaps you do not jot down each random act of kindness or each time you hold the door for someone or each time you give another a well-deserved compliment. By all means, however, you continue to do these things. The reality is that these little things will open your mind and heart to the bigger acts of generosity. In essence, while the little things are not worth journaling, they do matter.

THE GIVING JOURNAL

Thoughts From Social Media

Social media applications such as LinkedIn, Facebook, and Twitter has serve to expand our networks far and wide with lightning speed. As a result, we are able to gain ideas and insights from around the world. In that spirit, I asked the following question on various channels of social media and got the answers listed below.

Why do Net Givers end up getting more than Net Takers? Net Givers (those who are focused on giving first) get more than the person who is almost singularly focused on getting for themselves. While this seems counterintuitive, I see it holding true with rare exception. The question is why does it work this way?

Sabine Brandt, Chief Transformation Officer
Nobility Coaching & Consulting, Inc.
Plymouth, Minnesota

I believe that when one gives without expecting anything in return and with the attitude that there is enough for everyone, the receiving takes care of itself. Why does it work this way? Because when we selflessly bless others they will more often than not remember us for our goodness and our own blessings will find us in unexpected ways and often when we have long forgotten about what it was we gave in the first place.

Acts 20:35 "...it is more blessed to give than to receive."

Proverbs 11:25 "The generous will prosper; those who refresh others will themselves be refreshed."

Cristina Falcão
Portuguese Technical Translator
Lisbon, Portugal

Because people see that those are the ones that truly care about the others. It is the givers gain, the more you give the more you gain.

When you give expecting, no return, people feel they owe you something, not because you made them think so, but because you did not do that; in not doing it you get into people's hearts, and minds.

Tom Fish, Managing Director
Go Beyond, LLC
Springfield, Virginia

The universal Law of the Harvest says "you reap what you sow." You can't get out of something more than you put into it. Sure, you can have a temporary net gain, where you think you got more than you gave. Conversely, you can walk away feeling that you didn't get as much as you gave. But over time things tend to average out. Those who invest their time and energy (as well as their money) in activities that help others will get the most benefits.

Overall net givers come out ahead because generally you can't get out more than you put in. A net-taker can win on occasion and a net-giver can lose on occasion, but overall you reap what you sow. If you keep trying to take out more than you put in, sooner or later the Universe will get you.

Madrixo Levorne, Graphic Designer
Multiple Freelance Sources
Kaluga, Russia

Because of the natural award system. Life rewards automatically those who bring value, whether in giving or creating, whatever you do good will do more good for others and return to you much more than you invested. It's simple as that really.

Lisa Raymond, Owner
Deseyner's Eye Creations
Glendale, Arizona

You have accumulated many answers for your question, Frank, and many good points. One question you posed in your response to Mr. Griffith intrigued me - it has always intrigued me: "Do you give to get, or get to give?"

Net-givers help with no thought of their own gain, no thought of "how will this pay me forward in the future" attitude. They are focused on what they deem to be "the right thing", as interpreted and perceived through their experiences - not what they are told, but rather, what they feel. Net-givers are seen as trusted resources: known for their knowledge and expertise, liked for their generosity. People feel compelled to help net-givers in an effort to return this act of generosity. In order to be helped, you must first be willing to help.

"When you are nice to people, they want to be nice back to you." (Jack Canfield, 'Chicken Soup For The Soul'). As you give, you demonstrate how much you care about those around you and their success. People are drawn to this demonstration and want to know more about you, to find some way to help you. This unexpected act of "pay it forward" is their thank-you to you.

Matthew Sabath, Owner
Crazy Parrot Labs
Kirbyville, Missouri

I feel that it is because when you help another person, it brings a spirit of cooperation between the two parties. When relationships are synergistic, it builds upon itself. If I can help you achieve your goal, you will be more likely to help me achieve mine. It's all about the power of relationships and helping each other.

Yuhannes Watts, Chief Linking Officer
Learn2Link
Washington D.C.

Great Questions - it comes down to energy and an intention to help. If you help others, they are more likely to come back to you.

I give away a lot of help and a lot of free advice... I also get a lot of recommendations and referrals. This has to be something a person believes in and makes it their personal philosophy. Energy - you've got to put good energy out there in the world to get a lot of good energy back.

Whenever I begin a new relationship I imagine a huge black pot in between us. I always want to be the "first" person to put in that pot... I want to put so much into that pot that when I eventually need something and need to take a "scoop" out of that pot.. I want that scoop to have nice big chunks of meat and potatoes. Not just broth that filters out of the spoon. It goes beyond putting good energy into a relationship - this goes towards a larger good, a universal good.

I go out into the world everyday looking for opportunities to put out good energy and helping... this means telling someone that their outfit looks good, I like their tie, hold doors open for people, being kind and making others look good.

For the "getters" out there... well they get a few deals in the beginning... but others can quickly sense their energy and see that they aren't out to put into the situation. Networking is a long distance sport.. not a sprint. Those who are truly committed to helping others will win at the finish line. It a universal law that always holds true.

JOURNAL
Date   Act of Giving

JOURNAL

Date			Act of Giving

JOURNAL

Date   Act of Giving

JOURNAL

Date　　　Act of Giving

―――　　―――――――――――――――
―――　　―――――――――――――――
―――　　―――――――――――――――
―――　　―――――――――――――――
―――　　―――――――――――――――
―――　　―――――――――――――――
―――　　―――――――――――――――
―――　　―――――――――――――――
―――　　―――――――――――――――
―――　　―――――――――――――――
―――　　―――――――――――――――
―――　　―――――――――――――――
―――　　―――――――――――――――
―――　　―――――――――――――――
―――　　―――――――――――――――
―――　　―――――――――――――――
―――　　―――――――――――――――
―――　　―――――――――――――――
―――　　―――――――――――――――

ABOUT THE AUTHOR
FRANK J. AGIN

Frank Agin is the founder and president of *AmSpirit Business Connections,* an organization that empowers entrepreneurs, sales representatives and professionals to become more successful through networking.

As *AmSpirit Business Connections* has grown, Frank has established himself as an authority on professionals networking and business relationship development. He has written various articles on professional networking, is a sought after presenter on this topic (including using social media in business) and consults with companies and organizations on how to make a more effective use of business relationships.

Finally, Frank is the author of a book entitled *Foundational Networking: Creating Know, Like & Trust For A Lifetime of Extraordinary Success*, and is also the co-author of *LinkedWorking: Generating Success of the World's Largest Professional Networking Website* and *The Champion: Finding The Most Valuable Person In Your Network.*

Along with having a CPA designation, he has an undergraduate economics and management degree from Beloit College

(Beloit, Wisconsin) and an MBA and law degree from the Ohio State University.

He invites you to share your story of Giving with him. Contact him via e-mail (frankagin@amspirit.com) or LinkenIn at (www.LinkedIn.com/in/frankagin).

You can find his books at http://www.frankagin.com/

LinkedWorking:
Generating Success on the World's Largest Professional Networking Website

"Success on LinkedIn follows all the same rules as traditional networking."

LinkedWorking is a professional development book aimed at helping individuals achieve great success on LinkedIn, the world's largest professional networking website. Released March 2009.

Praise for *LinkedWorking*:

LinkedWorking is a great rubber meets the road to networking on LinkedIn. Lewis and Frank have taken a straight-to-the-point approach to online networking and how it will expand your horizons professionally and personally. I highly recommend you read and act on the advice in this book.

Gary Unger, Author
How To Be A Creative Genius (in five minutes or less)

Foundational Networking: Building Know, Like and Trust To Crete A Lifetime of Extraordinary Success

"Become the person you want to network with."

Foundational Networking is a personal development book aimed at helping people become better networkers by simply having better attitudes and habits. Released October 2008.

Praise for *Foundational Networking*:

Anyone who has read any of my books or articles knows that my ongoing themes are building one-on-one relationships, creating trust and credibility with everyone you touch, and serving others through the mantra of 'What goes around, comes around'. Frank Agin's book, Foundational Networking, beautifully, simply and effectively addresses all three through his concepts of presence, altruism and integrity in order to help you become the kind of person with whom you yourself would like to associate.

Dr. Tony Alessandra, Author
The Platinum Rule and *Charisma*

The Champion: Finding the Most Valuable Person in Your Network

"Who Is The Most Valuable Person In Your Network?"

Are you looking for a Champion? Don't you sometimes wonder: "There must be someone out there who will set me up with all sorts of great ideas, wonderful opportunities, and incredible new contacts, so as to bring me the success I deserve." If this is your dream, you've come to the right place. Destiny has brought you just a click away from the book that will help you find such an individual – The Champion. Released March 2010

Praise for *The Champion*:

Frank and Jim have woven a masterful tail that chronicles one networker learning a most important lesson.

When networking today it's no longer about what you know, who you know or even who knows you. What matters most now is how you're known. Almost by accident Jerry has the opportunity to change how he is known.

The lead character finally understands that being interested in others makes you far more interesting to them then actually trying to be interesting. I really enjoyed how they used the story of Jerry becoming the networking champion he sought to bring the success from networking we all seek.

Terry Bean
Founder Motorcityconnect.com and networkedinc.com

CPSIA information can be obtained at www.ICGtesting.com
Printed in the USA
BVOW010119111012

302559BV00001B/2/P

On Your Mark, Get Set, Go!

by Mary Dylewski

Harcourt
SCHOOL PUBLISHERS

Orlando   Austin   New York   San Diego   Toronto   London

Visit *The Learning Site!*
www.harcourtschool.com

Introduction

Look at the children on the cover of this book. They are pretending to be sprinters. A sprinter is a fast runner. Some sprinters can run 100 meters (109 yards) in less than 10 seconds! Now look at the swimmer on this page. He can swim 100 meters in about a minute. Where do sprinters and swimmers get their energy? Like you, they get it from food. But where does the energy in food come from?

Swimmers need energy to move through the water. ▼

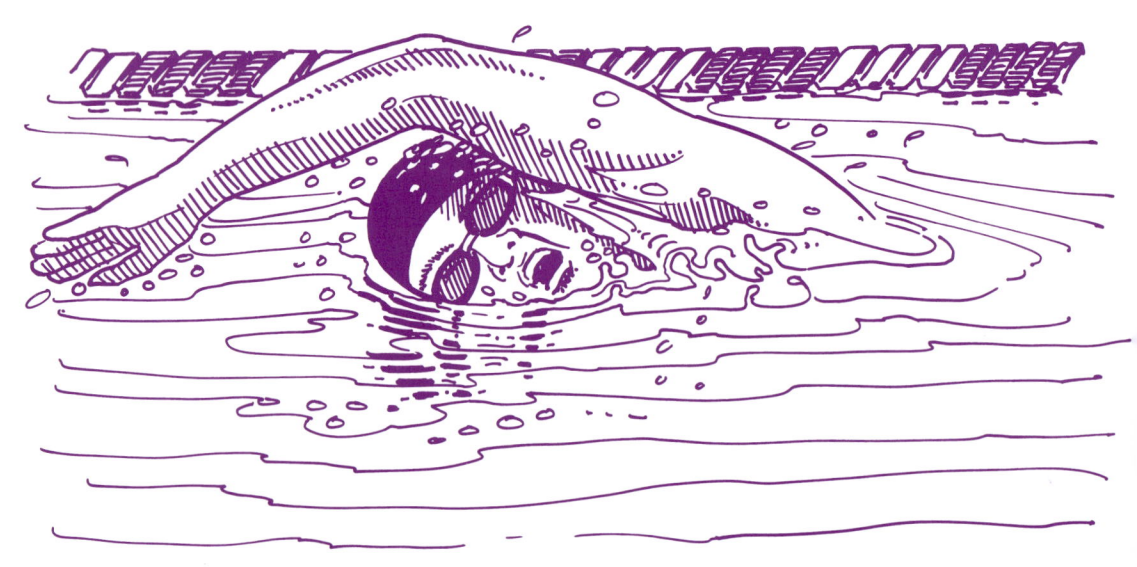

▼ Plants use energy from the sun to make food.

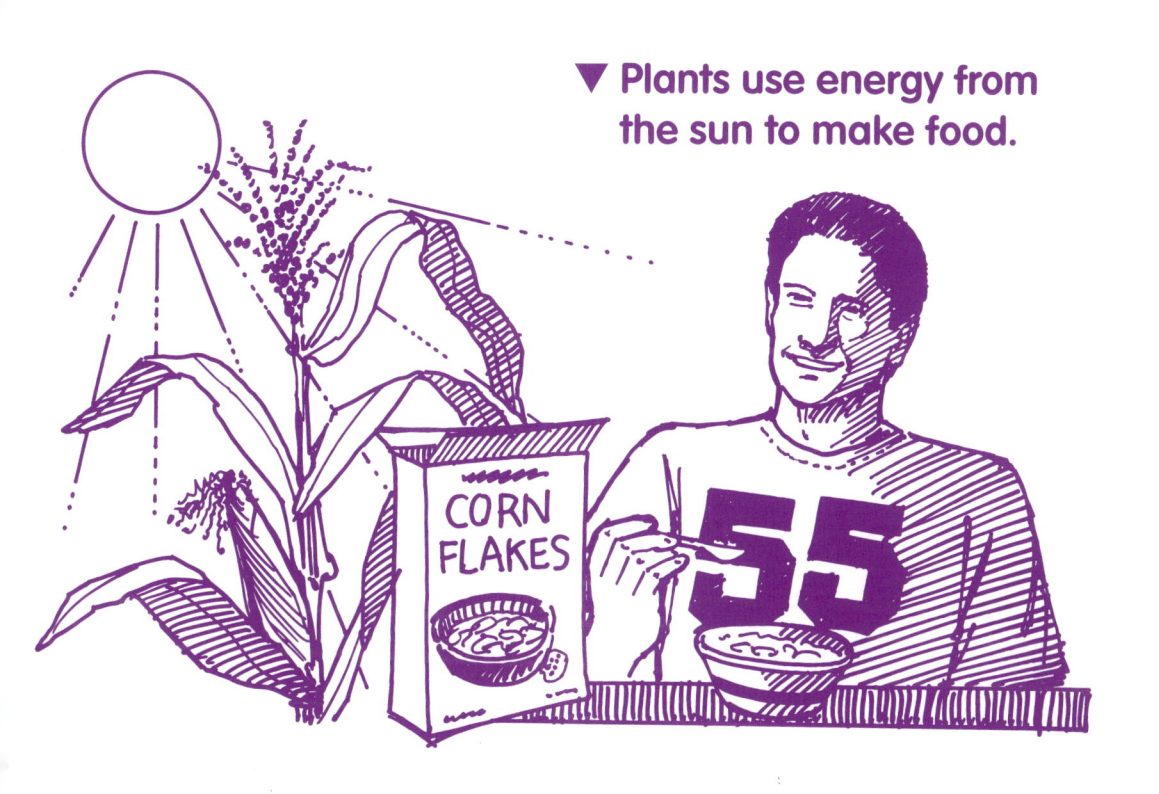

Energy from the Sun

The energy in food comes from the sun. Plants use the sun's energy to make their own food. They use some of this food to live and grow. They store the rest in their leaves, stems, roots, and fruits. The stored food has energy. When animals and people eat plants, they get energy from the sun. When people eat animals that eat plants, they get the energy those animals got from the sun.

Energy in Foods

Foods have different amounts of energy. Most athletes eat many kinds of food. This helps them get the energy they need.

Starches and Sugars

Starches have a lot of energy. Rice and pasta are starches. Sugars have a lot of energy, too. Fruits and milk are good sources of sugar. Starches and sugars digest quickly and easily. These foods give an athlete quick energy.

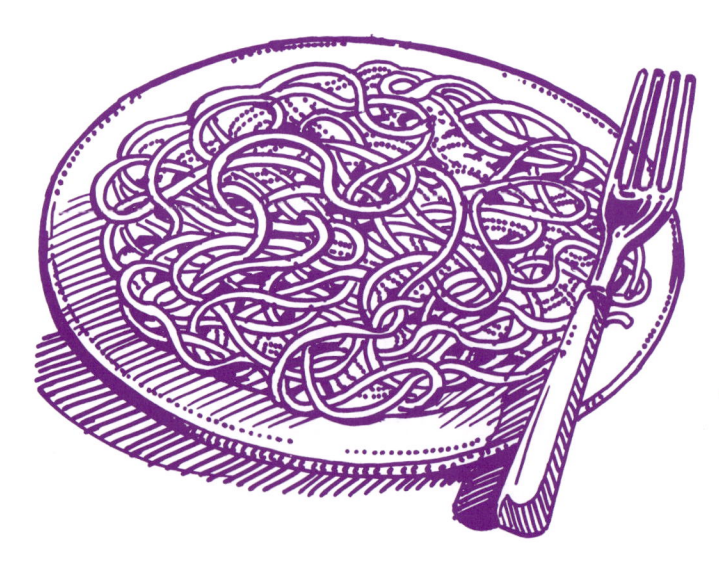

◀ Spaghetti is a type of pasta.

Protein

Proteins are also good sources of energy. They have about as much energy as starches and sugars. Eggs, milk, meat, and fish are high in proteins. Usually about one-fifth of an athlete's diet is protein.

Fats

Fats have a lot of energy. They have about two times as much energy as other foods. The body uses fats very slowly. So athletes do not eat fats for quick energy. Olive oil, nuts, and cheese are good sources of fat.

These foods are good sources of protein. ▼

Calories

Calories are units used to measure the energy in food. Some sports take more energy than others. So, some athletes need to eat more calories. A tennis player uses more calories than a sprinter. A skater uses more calories than a diver. A skier uses more calories than an athlete who races sleds over icy tracks.

Because they are active, athletes use a lot of energy. Most need at least 2,000 calories a day. Some need many more calories to train and perform well.

Digestion

People can't use the energy in food until the food is broken down into tiny bits. Then the body can take in the energy it needs from the food.

Breaking down food is called digestion. Digestion starts in the mouth. Teeth grind food into small pieces. These pieces go to the stomach. There, digestive juices break down the food even more. From the intestines, food enters the blood. The blood carries the food to all parts of the body. The body uses the energy to live, grow, and repair itself.

The body must digest food before the food can be used. ▶

- mouth
- esophagus
- stomach
- large intestine
- small intestine

Performance

An athlete's energy level needs to be high when the athlete is competing. Before an event, an athlete often eats a small meal of about 500 calories. Much of the meal is starches and sugars. These foods are easy to digest. They give an athlete quick energy.

During a short event, many athletes drink water or sport drinks. If the event is longer, athletes need more energy. Then they drink juices or eat fruits. Some athletes also eat proteins and starches when they compete.

During a race, many athletes drink water or sport drinks. ▼